The Scot's Little Instruction Book

The Scot's Little Instruction Book

Tony Sweeney

Thorsons
An Imprint of HarperCollins*Publishers*

To Connor, Amy & Nicholas, with love.

Thorsons
An Imprint of HarperCollins*Publishers*
77– 85 Fulham Palace Road,
Hammersmith, London W6 8JB
1160 Battery Street
San Francisco, California 94111–1213

Published by Thorsons 1996
1 3 5 7 9 10 8 6 4 2

© Tony Sweeney 1996

Tony Sweeney asserts the moral right to
be identified as the author of this book

Text illustrations by Bill Stott

A catalogue record for this book
is available from the British Library

ISBN 0 7225 3328 4

Printed in Great Britain by
HarperCollinsManufacturing Glasgow

Don't wear a kilt when bungee jumping.

 Buy a lottery ticket.

 Remember we're a' Jock Tamson's bairns.

 Stay happy, don't listen to the weather forecast.

Respect your mother and father.

 Buy a pair of wellies and an umbrella.

 Remember a plate of porridge a day keeps the doctor away.

 Visit your granny.

Acquire a kilt.

 Fit a padlock to your sporran.

 Never read the recipe for haggis.

 Holiday in Scotland at least once.

Adopt a Northern European perspective.

 Be proud of your accent – wear it like a badge.

 Don't drink tea with your pinkie in the air.

Roam in the gloamin with a lassie by your side.

 Invest in a good tent, rucksack and sleeping bag.

 Take a distillery tour and taste the wares.

Wear something tartan on November 30.

 Play spot the Tory MP.

 Don't drink and drive.

 Learn to ski.

Never trust a man who falls asleep
thinking about sheep.

 Believe in Willie Winkie.

 Put guid health before wealth.

 Hunt for Nessie.

Sledge in the local golf course.

 Be knowledgeable about Scottish history and geography.

 Always buy your round.

 Dae the slosh wae your mammy.

Don't wear your best suit to a Burns Night.

 Don't confuse capital punishment with a day out in Edinburgh.

 Don't wear a Celtic strip near an Orange Walk.

Don't steal osprey eggs.

 Oppose haggis culling.

 Like John Logie Baird – be inventive.

 Use your vote.

Don't call a minister 'father' unless he's your dad.

 Don't wear a Rangers strip near a Hibs Walk.

 Buy *Oor Wullie* and *The Broons* annuals.

Never believe the letters in the *Sunday Post*.

 Spend a September weekend in Blackpool.

 Only save what you cannae spend.

When in Glasgow spend Sunday at The Barras.

 Rent a salmon beat for the day.

 Play spot the location while watching *Taggart*.

Learn at least one folk song.

 Support local charities.

 Respect other cultures.

 Eat haggis, neeps and champit tatties on January 25.

Do Billy Connolly impersonations.

 Don't practise tossing the caber in the living room.

 Build snowmen.

 Go to a ceilidh in the Western Isles.

Don't talk to train spotters.

 Buy yersel a but-and-ben.

 Don't dance round your girlfriend's handbag.

 Buy a Scots dictionary.

Don't put a kebab in your good suit pocket.

 Plan to be in Paradise a half an hour before the Devil knows you are deid.

 Don't confuse a fiddlers' rally with a used car dealers' convention.

Learn to recognize unmarked Police cars.

 Wash at least once a day.

 Never go up a close to see a man aboot a dug.

 Set aside time to think.

Give up your seat for the elderly or infirm.

 Buy the *Big Issue*.

 Visit Edinburgh Castle.

 Have no time for bigots.

Acquire the Complete Works of
Robert Burns.

 Welcome tourists with a smile.

 Walk the West Highland Way for charity.

 Fly from your local airport.

Don't try to understand the Complete Works of Robert Burns.

 Remember 'A man's a man for a' that'.

 Own a copy of the Corries' Greatest Hits.

 When abroad, remember you are an ambassador for Scotland.

Support International Exhibitions held in Scotland.

 Where e'er ye be let your wind gang free.

 Don't call your weans Cyril or Percy (especially if they are girls).

 Never leave your pals behind.

If you emigrate, join the Caledonian Society.

 Remember a hot toddy is good for the body.

 Have a good lawyer.

 Picnic in the hills.

Carry a midge repellant.

 Climb at least one Munro.

 Never abuse other people's religion.

 Take a crash course in Gaelic.

Climb the Wallace Monument.

 Leave only your footprints on the hills.

 Remember money's round to go round.

 Visit your local Highland Games.

Spare a thought for others – learn to play the bagpipes in a soundproof room.

 Go out of your way to help people who are lost.

 Don't confuse a Highland fling with a dirty weekend in Inverness.

Lead by example – practise what you preach.

 Build networks – share information, ideas and experiences.

 Carry black bun and shortbread when first footing.

Never dilute the Water of Life.

 Never go wind surfing on Loch Ness.

 Walk on Culloden Moor.

 Be patriotic.

Don't piss in the sink in bed and breakfast accommodation.

 Buy at least two sets of thermal underwear.

 Remember Bannockburn.

Use colloquial slang to confuse people.

 Never go fishing in Loch Ness.

 Don't have your stag night near a main line railway station.

 Keep Scotland beautiful – attach satellite dishes to the back of your house.

Don't be afraid to greet in public – look what it's done for Gazza.

 Mind and put your wallies back in in the morning.

 Remember nothing should be worn under the kilt – exercise, to make sure it's all kept in good working order.

Mind and take your wallies oot at night.

 Refuse nothing but blows.

 Be wary of people with short arms and long pockets.

 Always get a weather report when heading for the hills.

Camp in Glencoe.

 Sample the pleasures of the Granite City.

 Don't eariewig into others' business.

 Enjoy buskers and always leave a donation.

Have a wee golden swally when you're feeling peely-wally.

 Like Bruce and the spider, if at first you don't succeed try, try and try again.

 Each year take two weekend breaks in different Scottish locations.

Don't clap scabby dugs.

 Do Sean Connery impersonations.

 Fight racism.

 Join a hillwalking club.

Always mean, speak and do well.

 Share your bawbees aboot.

 Share the crack with your mates.

 Beware of breengers.

Be selective – remember ten minutes of pleasure could mean a lifetime of misery.

 You've twa lugs, twa een and yin gub – use them in that proportion.

 Never overstay your welcome.

 Bodyswerve balloons and bampots.

Cuddle your loved ones at least once a day.

 Learn the art of slingin deifies.

 Never lumber your pal's maw.

 Bring in The Bells with family and friends.

Learn to recognize a rubber ear.

 Roam the ramparts of Stirling Castle and walk in the footsteps of great heroes.

 Read the Declaration of Arbroath.

 Learn the words of 'Auld Lang Syne'.

Don't go to the Post Office on giro day –
unless you've got one.

 Don't sing at your own wedding.

 Buy a Scottish international shirt.

 Leave offensive messages hidden in your
midden for the midgie rakers.

Visit the Forth Railway Bridge and wonder at the achievement.

 Live life to the full.

 Sit on Arthur's Seat and gaze on the sights below.

 Put up a birdbox.

Research your family tree and contact newly discovered relatives.

 Don't confuse Silicon Glen with Pamela Anderson's cleavage.

 Never budget for cheap fuel bills.

Learn 'Flower Of Scotland' and sing it with pride.

 Be proud of your heritage – learn of ancient heroes.

 Don't get pissed on the piste.

Invest in a good willie warmer.

 Chase your dreams – shoot for the moon.

 Invest in a good wooden cludgie seat.

 Always lift and lower the cludgie seat at the right times.

Never buy your scud books in your local town.

 Put valuables down your socks when going through rough areas.

 Avoid cadgers like the plague.

 Read the works of Sir Walter Scott.

Have a safe plank for your scuddies.

 Drive a hard bargain – anything is better than a Lada.

 Educate yourself – the tongue is mightier than the sword.

 Extend Scottish hospitality to all.

Follow the Country Code.

 Spend a summer holiday island hopping and be the 'Lord of the Isles'.

 Don't go about looking as if someone's stolen your scone.

Walk your corgis near Balmoral when the Queen is in residence.

 Take the high road to Loch Lomond.

 Go on a walking tour and follow in the footsteps of the Bonnie Prince.

Learn when to haud yer wheesht.

 Take your weans to the shows over Christmas – if you don't have any, take someone else's.

 Wish visitors *ceud míle faílte*.

Develop cosmopolitan attitudes and tastes.

 Be wary of nippin a hairy – never trust the quality of light up the jiggin.

 Carry a sporran flask full of amber nectar.

Have your friends round for a Ruby Murray.

 Don't confuse the Paps of Jura with a Craighouse lassie's chest.

 Toast good health in Gaelic – *slàinte mhath.*

Remember you're not invisible when you're out on the randan.

 Learn to play golf.

 Study the history of the clans.

 Always be generous with your time.

Lend a helping hand to any poor wee souls.

 Don't howk your nose in public.

 Set aside a small amount each week and once a year make a substantial donation to a worthy cause.

Always have the right money for the bus.

 Remember mony a mickle mak's a muckle.

 Dae the time if you cannae pay the fine.

 Never ask for an oven-ready haggis.

Drink quality whisky from quality Edinburgh crystal.

 Don't get on a bus that's going to Brigadoon.

 If you're going fishing – you'll catch f' aw in Loch Awe.

Don't plan to paddle in Lochnagar.

 Have a piper play at your wedding.

 Remember Mother's Day.

 Play a round at the home of golf.

Take a trip doon the watter oan the Waverley.

 Always make your way home before the Scotch mist descends.

 Quit while you're ahead.

When visiting Arran don't disturb the sleeping warrior.

 Explore the wynds and back courts of Auld Reekie.

 Climb the Cobbler then rest and be thankful.

Change your notes to Bank of England before heading south.

 Don't try and lumber the Five Sisters of Kintail.

 Take control of your own destiny.

When you're travelling, take time out to enjoy the magnificent beauty.

 Be assertive not aggressive.

 Don't confuse a good steeplechaser with a Fair Isle jumper.

Have a party after The Bells.

 Be a role model.

 Never discuss religion with strangers.

 Don't import other countries' problems.

Always insist on value for money.

 Don't mess with Aberdeen Angus.

 Buy a poppy on November 11.

 Observe speed limits.

Become a culture vulture – visit the Edinburgh Festival.

 Read the *Scots Magazine*.

 Take foreign visitors to the Tattoo and pay for their tickets.

Look to the future but be mindful of the past.

 Campaign against pollution.

 When you're pleased with a service always leave a substantial monetary tip.

Cross the Arrochar Alps.

 Learn the secret of a good cup of tea.

 Join the Sydney Devine Appreciation Society.

 Never put sugar on your porridge.

Never forget your anniversary.

 Visit the white sands of Morar – but watch out for Morag.

 When you're dissatisfied with a service, make your only tip a suggestion for improvement.

Buy the Collins travel guide to Scotland.

 Follow the Tomintoul whisky trail.

 Research tartans before you wear them.

 Sing Andy Stewart numbers at weddings and parties.

Visit the Glenfinnan Monument.

 Join the National Trust for Scotland.

 Climb Ben Nevis on a summer's morning.

 Visit local folk festivals.

 Buy a house with a view.

Poaching can be expensive – always purchase a fishing permit.

 Go to a Scottish Cup final.

 Keep up to date – read the 'what's on' guides.

Purchase a 'Historic Scotland' season ticket.

 Give a friend a copy of Ena Baxter's Scottish Cookbook.

 Take in a game against the Auld Enemy at Murrayfield.

Don't confuse a Glesga kiss with a winch up Sauchiehall St.

 Have lochside barbecues.

 Never let anyone badmouth your country.

 Wear the sgian-dhu in your right sock.

Always use your duty free quota.

 Pray – never be afraid to ask the Big Man for a hand.

 Get married in full Highland dress.

 Learn to play the spoons.

Phone at the cheap rate.

 Brush your teeth before a date.

 Make Friday night the boys' night.

 Where there's a choice buy Scottish products.

Always speak your mind – tactfully.

 Take a journey on the *Flying Scotsman*.

 Cast your nets far and wide throughout life.

 Invest in a good camera and use it often.

Visit the Trossachs and see 'Scotland in miniature'.

 Treat the mountains with respect – be prepared, it can be winter any day.

 Always leave mountain bothys as you find them.

Travel the Strathspey line.

 After a hard day at the boozer, always find time for the family.

 Stick Alba plates on your car.

 Make a pilgrimage to Iona.

Go skinny dipping in lochs, but watch out for the kelpies.

 Gather in Braemar.

 Enjoy the pleasures of the countryside.

 Encourage people to visit Scotland.

Know and observe the Mountain Code.

 Do the Castles tour.

 Join a menage.

 Always buy the best quality but try to purchase in the sales.

Make a trip to the Misty Isle.

 Help preserve the delicate balance between man and nature.

 Don't look for divisive issues but rather focus on the common bonds that unite the Scottish people.

Tour the abbeys and great houses of the Borders.

 Oppose nuclear dumping.

 Look for the good in people – it's always there, you just may have to do a little digging.

Remember you're creating tomorrow's history today.

 Do voluntary community work.

 Read W.H. Murray's books on Scotland.

 Pass down tales and legends.

Traverse the Great Glen and listen to the echoes of the past.

 If you have no clan connection wear the Caledonia tartan.

 Always mind that one good deed deserves another.

Don't be penny wise and pound foolish.

 Educate Sassenachs.

 Gather lucky white heather.

 Use picturesque postcards when dropping a line to family and friends.

Value the three f's – family, friends and faith.

 When travelling at night watch out for the spirit of the glen.

 Converse with your erse while travelling in the Highlands.

Never miss a bargain.

 Collect the Highlander films.

 Sample Loch Fyne oysters.

 Make your way to Stornoway – if it's Sunday mind and take a carry oot.

Protect the environment – deposit recyclables.

 Have a scotch & rye on Hogmanay.

 Join your local neighbourhood watch scheme.

 Visit the beaches of the Western Isles.

Keep a diary and learn from experience.

 Happiness is one of the few things that doubles every time you share it with someone – so spread it around.

 Avoid Rab C. Nesbitt's tailor.

 Never patronize friends or colleagues.

Don't confuse the Edinburgh Fringe with a dodgy haircut.

 Go on a Highland photo safari.

 Throw a scramble at weddings.

 Be alert to life's learning opportunities.

View problems as improvement opportunities.

 Always correct foreigners who refer to you as 'English'.

 Endeavour to do the best you can in everything you do.

Visit Royal Deeside and see the Monarch of the Glen.

 Be your own man – if you're married, be your wife's man.

 Don't hold a stag party on the glorious twelfth.

Carry a donor card.

 Don't confuse deer stalking with cheap lycra tights.

 Keep Scotland tidy – use litter bins.

 Keep fit in body and mind.

Don't sook Dumbarton Rock.

 Support your local boozer.

 Give compliments and praise where they are due.

 Always look on the bright side of life.

Bury the national tendency for lack of self-belief.

 Don't listen to English sports commentators.

 Visit national nature reserves.

 Lift your kilt at weddings and fancy dos.

Join the Tartan Army and restore the Hampden roar.

 Sample the delights of Scottish ales and brew.

 Claim to have seen 'The Monster' and fabricate wonderful stories.

Stand your mates a drink when they're skint.

 Don't let your dog foul public places.

 Ponder independence.

 Learn key swear words in Gaelic.

Grow heather in your garden.

 Carry a roll-up kagoul.

 Have a different balaclava for each day of the week.

 Always celebrate a new birth in style.

Follow the ten commandments.

 Invest in a pair of good quality walking boots.

 Leave a half out for Santa.

 Eat chips and curry sauce.

Be loud and boisterous, especially on holiday.

 Keep in touch with friends who move away.

 Go on camping expeditions with your kids, even if it's only in the back garden.

Bathe in the Gulf Stream.

 Visit Skara Brae and step back in time.

 Tramp the Gramps.

 Travel on the overnight sleeper to London.

Wear tartan boxer shorts.

 Get your priorities right, make your family your number one team.

 Adopt a canny attitude – don't buy what you cannae afford.

 Don't do drugs – expose the pushers.

Reject the shell suit culture – expose the pedlars.

 Scotland belongs to you and yours – enjoy and protect your ben and glen.

 Go on the ghost tours of Stirling and Edinburgh old town.

'The best laid plans o' mice and men gae aft agley', so always have an alternative.

 Sow your wild oats before you get married.

 Don't confuse a sgian dhu with a pigeon on the lecht.

Spend it if you've got it – it's only a mug who is poor in life and rich in death.

 Give thanks for the lassies.

 Remember good manners cost nothing but bad manners can cost you dearly.

 Discuss devolution.

Explore the great outdoors.

 Treat Scotland as a land of adventure.

 We're all one big family, so look out for each other.

 Spread the word – to buy this book.

Watch 'Scottish Women'.

 Lift up his kilt in public and bring a little colour to your man's cheeks.

 Don't confuse labour pains with your local district councillors.

Don't let your man near the family allowance book.

 Command respect from your partner. Learn a few key phrases from the Scottish language of love, e.g. 'Watch yer mouth, ya cheeky pig!' 'Make that yer last pint!' 'Hand over the money, pronto!'

Believe in love at first sight, but take a second look when you're sober.

 Learn the alley cat.

 Use your handbag to smuggle half bottles into weddings and functions.